Evolution's Promise

Meditations of a Magical Thinker

Evolution's Promise

Meditations of a Magical Thinker

Duane R. Johnson

Published by Smoky Hill
2650 SE Lake Terrace
Topeka KS 66605

http://www.viewfromsmokyhill.com

ISBN: 978-0-692-89204-6

Dedicated to Elvera, Heidi and Blake

Acknowledgements

Thanks to:

Becky Stone, my long-suffering sounding board, and great supporter.

The Beta Team, for catching those embarrassing mistakes, and making this a better book:
Phil Esau, Heidi Johnson, Blake Johnson, Raylene Heinz-Penner, Monica Schrag, Myles Schrag

---

Cover Design by award-winning artist Renee Barratt, http://www.TheCoverCounts.com

---

A Friendly Tip

These poems are meant to be read aloud
a few each evening just before bedtime
and savored with your favorite bedtime snack.

TABLE OF CONTENTS

Poet of Cocoons

Poetry, sometimes cocoon,
more often is ointment on a wound
called the human condition.
A fan of cocoons to ease transitions,
my suspicion is too much focus on the wound
leads to spiritual malnutrition.
So when I write, I spin cocoons
with a butterfly's ambition.

Some need salve to soothe the wound, I don't deny,
but if your embryonic spirit wants a loom
to weave a womb where it can lie
until you're ready for the sky
here am I, poet of cocoons
and midwife to your butterfly.

SHALOM

"God, let me speak in a way that glorifies you and edifies
the people around me."

– Glen Alexander Guyton

Woods, Lake and City

I remember woods that surrounded a lake
in a mid-sized city.
I remember a presence there
that taught me not to push.

It enveloped those woods that surrounded that lake
in this mid-sized city,
no other boundaries mattering.
It was a unifying force, drawing

every island of awareness stirring
within those woods and lake
into one singular presence, itself
a fractal of reality, a splendid being
in which to move and breathe, and the children
growing up in those woods by that lake in this growing city

glide comfortably through tight spaces
by signaling to neighbors
as they slalom through the dappled light.

Somewhere in the Water

For you, fishing is a science.
For me, it's art.

Perhaps that's why I catch fewer fish,
but I resist fishing by the numbers
because I mimic awkwardly.

True, sometimes I cast to pool or riprap
like any logical angler
and feel unseen tugs in the water,
same as you.
Like you, I bend the rod to pry
my hidden prize from the depths,
resisting its lure to meet halfway
and endure its baptism.

Still, my cast, while rippling shallows
you'd know better than visit,
curls from my left hand with graceful arc,
bearing my signature,
and I know you wouldn't have me change it for
        convenience's sake –
to catch more fish,
to feed the multitudes,
to bring abundance to the market,
or even to save the whales.

Floating flies and wading boundaries
has become my favorite pursuit.
The art of fishing explores shorelines nature mandates
then bends them to allow each cast
that doesn't harm the water.

When art and science meet, lines tangle.
At any moment, I expect your unseen tug,
resisting, trying to reel me toward you.

It will take courage for both of us
to meet half-way,
somewhere in the water.

Tightening the Seam

It just felt like something was going to happen.
Maybe the way leaves barely quivered
and how the alpenglow recast its golden hue on the stage.
Certainly there was something in Jerry's voice on "Ripple"
as the crowd, now quiet, leaned toward him.

It's then that I felt them stir in both brain and breast:
those mystic threads of intimacy, drawing
everyone closer, tightening the seam.

It happens countless times in life,
beginning with an intimation that we'd better pay attention
or miss some blessed event.
Cues and outcomes are never the same,

but the stirring of those threads through brain and breast
always tweaks our senses just before the moments tighten
and as every soul around us draws closer to the seam
we can see in their eyes they feel it, too.

Readily Accessible

There's a readily accessible rocky point that seems
    promising to fishermen.

Seldom is,
and on this mild and still Thanksgiving Friday
God, seemingly content with listing beside me,
is granting me the grace to not let rainbows bother me
so as to spend these moments teaching me
the purpose for eternally being –
perfecting the art of interacting with each other.

That's why we're prone on this rock, me with jacket
    unzipped,
surveying this small piece of His great acre
as close as striders to water.

Across the lake, 500 yards away
riveting our attention, bicyclists,
passing an orange jogger,
bee-lining like ants below the looming lamps
and blue-lit scoreboard of a diamond

gliding toward that strolling family of five
about to disappear into a clutch of hickories.

Countless times I've strode that quarter mile
and know its penchant for collisions. So we're wondering,
what will the family of five deliver in the clutch?
Will the bikers brake-and-go as the clutch allows?

Perhaps we'll hear something.
We'll let you know.

Campground Fox

He came out from the brush at a casual trot
never guessing an intruder was already watching him.
I wondered how close he'd come before he spotted me
and was a bit surprised he never did.

Arms up, I glanced him off.
He yelped, nearly leapt off the cliff on his right
then found a favorable curve away from me.

We've seen each other several times since,
always conceding space,
treating each other with mutual respect,
keeping a casual distance.

Getting Struck by That Thought

Did you just get struck by that thought?
Did I glimpse it propel from this maple above us
and smack you as you glanced askance?

A thought is what I think it was,
the kind our favorite poet saluted
when he asked, "Why
are there trees I never walk under
but that large and melodious thoughts
descend upon me?"

Large and melodious.
I think that's the kind of thought it was,
not that I've ever thought thoughts quite like that.

But the poet was well acquainted with such thoughts.
By the time he posed his question, "Why…?"
he'd moved on to seeking origins,
tracing his conclusions' breadcrumbs
backward to his soul.

Getting struck by that thought
must have been a pleasant collision.
Congratulations, and consider your good fortune.
I guess it's my dumb luck the thought missed me,
but you can pass it on in verse for me to savor.

As well as I, you understand
that poetry is your body and soul conversing
the way you'd like others to speak with you,
honestly, generously, joyfully,
like your sister to her lover.

So, share that thought that struck you,
and let's see if I can find its twin
dangling from this branch above me.

Perhaps we'll trot these brother-sister thoughts in tandem, and know each other better.

Seminal Moment

What harm can come from stepping in the way
except perhaps to me?

I watch some stranger's
ragged children playing,
then turn to see my neighbors
lurching forward
clenching teeth and clutching stones,
like chimpanzees, snarling
at the children,
hurling insults,
"Heathens! Miscreants! Little savages."

Enraged, they hurl their stones,
and I step into the gap,
watching missiles close
on frightened children praying
and on me.

What harm is done
by stepping in the way?

Halfway Through the Hike

Red foxes have short memories, Samuel.
If we stay silent, he'll come back
to give this glen a sharper look.

So, how're your soybeans? Past the hump?
I'm no farmer, but I see how headers can be headaches.
At least you cleared a forty before our congregation called.

Samuel, at these prices, driving sixteen hundred miles
is more than distantly expensive. And to share
three hours of your metered wit
allotted over several days!
I take on faith that you were paid
in something more divine than wages.

You know I embarrass some
when they see me turn transparent.
I'll be open because you know as well
that both of us are more than halfway through the hike,
and tomorrows are uncertain –
notwithstanding premonitions glimpsed
while resting here, near our children's Ebenezer.

You helped me teach mine
how to clutch their captain's compass to their hearts
to reach this rugged land whose king
is better thought of as a father.
I've heard you muse about the danger this king poses
to kings of lesser realms
because he calls us all his sons and daughters.
These lesser rulers know that kinsman's bonds
are stronger than the strongest walls they build
to hem their borders.

So, be my witness as I pledge allegiance
to this nation you blazed your trail to pioneer

so many years ago. Til now,
I've been your visitor and guest.
Today, I ask to be your fellow countryman.
Test me how you will, you'll find me ready.

I've lived a skeptic's life too long.
My sins, stones I've lifted from the trail,
lay heavy in my pack.
I trust that you can understand
and overlook my lagging stride
to greet me with your patient smile
as I struggle to catch up.

When we were just below the summit,
as so often is the case on steep inclines
once the air becomes too rare
for Bristlecone and Ponderosa,
the valley we'd just risen from
became the hour's panorama.
Did you notice how meandering turns
and folded tucks of earth obscured
the best and worst along the eroded trail
that bore the boot-prints of our climb?

I considered it divine relief
that we were spared the sight
of certain steeples as we neared the Peak.
It embarrasses me to know the veils
that screen the holiest of holies
in such less-than-sacred temples
are banners of their lesser realms.
I've no way of fathoming your thoughts, Samuel,

but I've watched you wince and blush as well;
we've both seen misplaced banners planted
in too many houses of the holy.
The true king's breath blows through such flimsy fabric,
then leaves it lifeless.

But, here, three blue concentric circles
fly in every corner of this sanctuary.
I stand, salute, whisper psalms of praise, then pray
– then hurry to catch up again;
regardless of the trail's incline,
the faster fellow-travelers move the quicker we must be.
But be quick carefully;
adjust at every switchback or get lost,
or worse, go tumbling into Devil's Playground.

Look, the fox is back. We'll see
how good that squirrel's memory is.
Oh! No memory now!
The little fellow never saw him coming.
Anticlimax though it seems
I'd guess the fox's fee was paid
in something less divine than wages
but just as sacred to the fox.

I'd like to stay and linger, Samuel,
but the entertainment's over
and we have no more excuses.
Unless we finish with this hike
we'll find no better end,
because around this fork the foxes are too active.

It's time to go our separate ways for several seasons.
Our clans will plan to gather once again
when next year's soybeans green your fields,
here, where our favorite mountain climbs above us.

Til then, stay healthy, Samuel, laughing
with your neighbors, sing loudly
in your hermitage on wheels,
and plough your furrow straight until next summer.

FAITH

"Natural value may occasionally be created accidentally and without purpose. But when a process produces a progressive, interdependent structural chain of value, which increases in magnitude and intensity consistently across vast stretches of space and over huge spans of time, we must recognize it as purposive. Explaining this universal process as purposeless or otherwise accidental ignores the evolutionary evidence and ultimately defies reason."

– Steve McIntosh, *Evolution's Purpose*

In the Falling Snow

It's the chicken-or-egg dilemma.
I pondered this most recently on Sunday
when, while fishing for distraction
from a cancerous prognosis, it began to snow.
Flakes meandered down until they melted
in the river to begin another cycle.

Or, does the cycle end with river flowing
so that the circle re-circles when
water turns to vapor? Or,
is the final segue vapor rising?

These thoughts were still revolving when
the start of darkness sent me home to sleep. Then
dawn on Monday awoke me with
the answer, which I immediately forgot, and now,
once more, I'm in the dark about which phase
is the start.

But regardless of what works
I do or fail to do six months to a year from now,
this simple fact, at least, I know:
my faith is in the falling snow
whether it bring ending or
beginning.

Lightning Surging

Relax with me to contemplate astronomers,
like Kepler and Copernicus, examples
of creation glancing back to contemplate itself,
to peer with awe and wonder through a peerless universe,
and then to pen new chapters in the tomes
of science, lightning surging through their veins.

Existence of the universe without awareness
of itself would be absurd, a hoax played on itself
if stars would only shine their light on minds
that can't reflect! So if you're searching for a purpose
to your life, know that self-awareness is
enough to justify each breath you take.

Yet, when we view the universe with reverence
resolve to wield its keys, then pledge our lives to keep
it safe, for rich or poor, in sickness and in health,
it bonds us to itself as its companions
on its splendid, endless journey through the mindful time
of God, his lightning surging through our veins.

Suspended in Eternity

Most ents look like oaks, you know,
except each one is its own designated driver,
the muscular momentum of their limbs etching
a carousel of sepia-toned silhouettes across a pale-ale sky.

I've strolled the quieter side of my favorite lake
for the sole purpose of watching them moving.

They dance in slow motion
– stop-action so it almost seems to me,
etching my own brief moment in time.
They dance with the joy of *anima movens* suspended in
　　eternity.
They dance unafraid of orcs and goblins that terrorize
oaks on winter nights.

And they dance because they know
that regardless of what things we think we see that might
　　be figments
the joy is real.

A Glass to Grace

I'm learning poetry is the sound of one soul spinning,
be it echoes of Escher climbing stairs
sweet James' run through fire and rain,
Michelangelo's more muted pyramid of pity
or a simple spinner thinking.

I've struggled my entire life to control my spin
half the time without a clue to where the ground is,
so I know mid-course corrections
would be easier if roll, pitch and yaw
could be voice-activated.

Not long ago, on the last work day of the week,
in a favorite restaurant, if only for a moment,
my voice seemed to center
in a blessing to grace, doorway to eternity.

So let's drink a glass to grace,
which grants us all the time we want
to practice the craft of living
the rest of today and tomorrow.

To grace, the breath that stirs this life we've been given,
just as joy and wonder serve as wings.

The question in the balance
is how we'll use this liberty grace affords us,
and on that point I know which way I pivot.

We would owe grace our allegiance for life alone,
but the gravity of its goodness draws us to it
in self-perceptual motion
boostered by our joy and wonder.

Embrace a God of Goodness

Embrace a God of goodness
and you escape the desert
God who teases you
with life
then snatches it from you.
No Creator whose nature is to love
would bestow one single breath
without offering eternity.

So, embrace a God of goodness
and Easter morning dawns
self-evident
your eye of faith confirming
the tomb is empty.
Indeed, all tombs are emptied
priceless contents claimed
not by worms
but by Spirit's flame.

Greater Part of Me

I think I'd like to die beneath a tree.

Just doze off some sunny April afternoon,
cat across my legs,
unpublished verse imprinted on my heart
and a breeze to lift my spirit.

In fact, I've already picked the tree,
a maple old enough to flame this autumn,
though still too young to sit beneath.

So, yesterday, I sat beneath a nearby tree,
pondering weighty matters that crowded out
all thoughts of my mortality.

Today, my mind less crowded,
I pray the greater part of me
will be aware of death beneath a tree
and greet it humbly.

In Angled Trinity

One still-born night while keenly gazing through black
(a shepherd to my blanket and campfire, stewing),
conversing with a planet, star and sliver of moon poised in
    angled trinity,
suddenly my sight was captured by a flyer,
appearing like a cat, bewitching me.
Darting with pinball grace, caroming
from rock to tree,
I chased the erratic specter half an hour, never moving,
all the while admiring its wings.

Perceiving its way with echoes of its own song,
it wandered between the canyon wall and Pegasus Square,
searching rocky crevices,
exploring Mercuric and lunar reflections,
curiously probing Sirius' pinpoint beam,
and carefully inspecting all the darkened time between.

Then something seemed to snicker in the wind,
piquing the creature's darker nature.
Emitting a wicked cry, an unspeakable sound,
it circled my head again and again,
each time winging closer, ever closer, menacing
like an omnipresent shadow.
Quick to my defense, a piece of cedar
hissed and popped amid the flame.

The next thing I remember
I was lying on the ground,
my memory of the past few hours hidden
with the trinity beyond unseen clouds.
Yet, something in the stillness
and my fire's steady glow
evoked again my concentrated gaze.
Instantly the fire surged and wrapped me in its light;
quietly its tongue revealed

spirit-tempered insight.

"There are times," the glowing cedar whispered,
"when even miracles cannot convince;
dark nights when zephyrs, faithful dawn to dusk,
are fooled by demons dressed in black
and snicker at the perfect art of God.
Work hard to fuel your fire then;
its heat can blunt doubt's penetrating power,
its light will separate seekers from shadows,
its choir of vowel-less sounds will summon your seraphim
who stands prepared to guide you
with the compass fastened to his wings."

Then, as it touched me with its final blaze,
I tossed more kindling on the cedar's ember,
lay back with arms outstretched
to witness to the lifting haze,
and made confession to the planet, star and sliver of moon.

While all about me, quiet reigned,
mosquitoes popped above my flame,
which sparked the dark for things unnamed,
climbing the trinity's spiraling lane upward
toward the still-point's plane
to find within its coal-sack pitch
the purest light of ecstasy.

Windsailor

I've known the man since he was young.
Back then, he reached away full sail,
from islands of solid thought.
Still, though it annoyed him to admit his fear
he tried to hold fast to his Wind-driven task
of believing.

His ignorant allegiance graduated
through a few degrees
of pain. Still, faith stayed, and he began,
in autumn's sun-drenched blush, to hear
and learn to catch his spirit's zephyr
and hone the craft of seeing

what good science can't ignore.
Now, he ploughs his seas of faith, close-hauled
toward his finest thought,
and more often is it becoming clear
that making fluid transitions is
the art of sailing.

PAST

"If you wish to make an apple pie from scratch, you must first invent the universe."

– Carl Sagan, *Cosmos*

Deathwatch

She wore a bluebird on her chest,
new blue plumage, rusted breast;
twigs adorned with spring-fresh blossoms
clutched in twisted bird-fists.

She throated counter-pointed tunes,
first warbling of him in past tense,
then singing of his Christmas plans,
cocking ear and eye
to listen for his breath
and watch for heaving in his chest.

He caught her eye,
then caught his breath enough to rasp,
"Go home and be about your business, hon,"
then closed his eyes
and folded fists across his chest.

Tennessee Tulips

In Tennessee, tulips grow at heights
you can't reach,
on trees that spear the air a dozen feet
before they branch and bud;
blood-red buds
unfurling green blunt-end leaves
to form perimeters around
the orange and yellow petals they protect.

In Tennessee, I grew to manhood
without observing
– until that second time
my heart was breaking –
lovelier tulips grew at heights
I could not reach.
To save my heart a fatal break
I learned to love them
from a distance, enduring
until their fragrance
filtered downward.

What wisdom I've gleaned
I owe to tulips
beyond my reach in Tennessee.
"Look at the tulips," someone says,
and you look down,
unless you've grown
to cherish tulips
beyond your reach in Tennessee.

Fountains of Calamine

Once I plucked some poison ivy,
not out of ignorance, but out of need,
the need to do a manly deed and proudly suffer.

Indeed I suffered,
suffered for a patch of woods whose future I'd forever
    altered,
forever changing God's acre with my tickled will.
And I wondered if my friends would love me any less
with all these blisters around my neck,
or if heaven held another patch for me to scratch in.

Then I prayed the world would be lovelier for my efforts,
prayed precaution's bud would blossom from the rash,
resolved humility would guide my boots as they come
    crashing down
where flowers might have grown,
and suddenly, the itching left my palms.

My Cemetery Days

For two years during the Nixon debacle, I worked at an appliance parts store within walking distance of a Memphis cemetery. Often, two or more of us would visit the cemetery during our lunch breaks.

We would eat, read epitaphs, climb trees, toss Frisbees, and get visited by police, who had been called by a resident of a home adjacent to the cemetery. He could not see why someone with no relatives in the cemetery would want to spend so much time there.

Recently, I rediscovered in an old notebook a few fragmented sentences that appear to have been my reply at the time. I reworked it into a short meditation that immediately prompted yet another reflection.

FUTURE

Emergence: "An inherent, energy-driven trend in evolution toward new levels of organization."

– Herbert Spencer

The Cemetery

What's there to fear in an acre of the dead?
Not this old, red oak, strange in form but quiet and clean.
Outside the cemetery's finial fisted fence,
Mad Horse Ash, with their itching parasites, sweep past
as fifty phantoms of gray on a passing train.

Is it possible to reach the shores of paradise fully cleansed?
Here's a hundred cairns that mark the worm-infested way
        of souls who tried.
Made it worth the rest.

Cemetery Commentary

I'm asking if it's possible to be perfect, or rather, to be
    perfected?

To begin, we have God, the original and archetype
    personality, always perfect.
Then there's all us little personalities
running around on a little dot
at the far end of a universe of universes.
We start out about as far removed from perfection as it's
    possible to be,
only to hear God challenge us
to perfect the art of living with each other – to be perfect.

Which, in our case, means getting there the hard way,
learning by doing and dinging elbows every step of the way.
And getting incrementally better one year at a time,
but destined by death to never come close to perfecting
    ourselves.
Then, at the end of reason,
we place faith in the grace of God
to grant us eternal time to learn to love each other.

Promising New Wonders

The night I die you'll see my soul,
a rainbow shroud around the moon,
promising flood tides as you watch blue oceans ebb,
promising new wonders washed ashore.

So, as you stumble along this beach at midnight,
casting glances toward me,
cast out, instead, toward salt-moist sand
strewn with starfish, castles and chambered shells,

and there, beneath my radiant shroud, you'll glimpse
an evolution in my death,
a greater breast to catch my breath,
and endless cycles gleaning.

Abraham's Salute

Toast with me what humankind will be
an evolution of heart, hand and brain from today.
I envy our begotten
seventy times seven generations
paid forward. Just as high, let's lift our mugs

to brothers and sisters who, with us, blazed
this planet's trail with courage and cunning.
I trust as we traverse the mansion worlds
that fringe the fulcrum of infinity,
nourishing our souls with lessons learned

from fellow pilgrims born on countless spheres,
the day will dawn when we will hear the news —
our sons and daughters back on Earth have breached
the outer limits of their DNA
to plot their soul-paths straight to Paradise.

Then I will pause to glance about the hills
of Salvington, recall the promise of Melchizedek
of seed to populate the stars
and muse about that dawn when light
will grant me my next grand epiphany.

Keep Moving

The future? There it comes again
folding itself into today
to pay tomorrow's wages.

Hope? This is its currency; tomorrow
time-travels wires of our desire
to energize the rising sun.

As concerns you now, the Son of man
is Father of your children – He stands
as witness before heaven of what mankind

is becoming. His footprints
you'll discover on the path emerging
from that very moment you dare

to tread upon it. History? Just a fusillade
of hollow shells fired from canons
of the dead. If you delay to search the bush

for leaflets littered long ago
you'll not be happy when shadows find you.
So, keep moving.

Above the Branching Sway

Dawn's flash is glimpsed beneath this flexing willow
as Venus winks above its branching sway.
So quick is the flight of this gypsy light,
dancing just a stretch away, lap away,
and Pegasus could take me there.

Wait for me lady, please,
mounted on Pegasus,
saddleless, quasar-quick,
memory guiding him,
gravity spurring him,
marveling, galloping, galloping,

The Twins

The chestnut and chinkapin are twins.
In youth, they galloped ent-speed
across this soft, green finger reaching
into water.

In summer, they settled down,
farmed the land,
and watched each other's children
into fall.

Now it's fall
and they're barely moving.
Beneath their roots they feel
the finger pulsing faster.
The twins are not concerned;
they trust the land
so they've never
feared fall.

They're simply taking in this lake
and knowing I'm as well.
As foliage turns, we trade reflections
on each pool we try to fathom.

Chestnut sometimes wonders
whether sparkles in the water
are coded conversations
with the sun.

Chink, the scientist of the two,
believes the sun is using water
to flash his code to us.

I always agree with both, despite my doubts,
because I share their faith
in an intelligent divine.

In fact, they swayed me
on our first good night together.
Often since, I've thought
I've seen one ripple wink at me
while I'm in prayer,
as if to say I have an audience
whose ear is quicker
than my voice.

When I return in twenty years
on a day when green is for a season
cloaked in white
and stroll the easy distance
past the finger's second knuckle

I'll find the twins still
bearing fruit, though noticeably bent,
having learned in intervening years
how to commune with sun and water to exhaustion.

They'll take me generously to boughs
and we'll muse about our children
as we watch the lake together
until sunset coaxes me
to leave.

Then the twins will turn
their quick attention to familiar darkness,
stretching leathery fingers
toward stars they've known since birth
and on their first good night,
befriended.

PRESENT

"Values ... did not come into being separately from the rest of existence; they are emergent in the evolution of the biosphere. We are the products of that evolution, and our values are real features of the universe."

– Stuart Kauffman, *Reinventing the Sacred*

Diminishing at Dawn *

I thought that dinosaur had died –
our midnight shadow on the prowl
too slow to catch our nimblest dreams,
until, diminishing at dawn
it'd slipped into la Brea's grip.

But no, its fossil haunts us still
an agony to those who'd hoped
we'd freed ourselves from savage times
and now, post-mortemism done,
had locked it in Smithsonian's cave.

But...
    no...
        the fossil...
            haunts us...
                still....

*Dedicated to our brothers and sisters at:
- Emanuel AME Church, Charleston, S.C.
- Tree of Life Synagogue, Pittsburgh, Pa.
- Pulse nightclub, Orlando, Fla. . . .

Beginning Deep

Sometimes it's a silent battle.

More often, the liquid mirror's surface shatters
and the rainbow rises with splash and spray
that is eight parts drama queen, six parts ballerina.
If the sum of the parts exceeds the whole
then even in dim light you know it's a rainbow.

In dim light is when it battles best
when, barely seen, it clearly sees its enemy:
red cap, tan coat, gray hip boots
anchored safe in water two feet deep
wind-blown face and furrowed brow
eyes focused on the rod bent double
except to cast a glance or two
at turmoil in the water.

From the whirlpool's eye, the rainbow
arches into alien air, by string entangled
with the angler in a dance of spooky action
and in that instant when
the surface shatters, you see them both,
attitudes slanted against each other
two hearts proud of their height
creating chaos in the water.

Then, sometimes there's that silent battle,
beginning deep
resisting its erratic ride toward the angler
only when the net is poised appearing
as though teleported from a league below.

And you never hear the rainbow.

At Certain Hours

Someone said I talk too much
at certain hours,
a point of view I took exception to
and though she watched me silently
I argued until the hour was over.

She seemed arrogant to me
and I figured her to be too quick to judge as well,
so I waited for her fangs to penetrate
my skin, injecting venom.

She waited several moments when I ended,
smiled and replied, "Your hour's over,"
retrieved the yellow project from her lap
and continued with her knitting.

Left with no alternative,
I used the silence to decode her meaning
then studied her unspoken words
and committed them to memory.

Dancing

Late last night
all lights out
in my hearth
along the back of a single piece of kindling
fire dancing to its own music

From the earth
silent shout
through the night
across the crown of a universe of universes
my mind dancing to its own musings

Out Here on Ice

The lake beneath this frozen shell
plunges deep as the sky I see
at its bottom.

I don't venture onto ice
because its natural for me to venture.
I'm a Cancer;
we like to nest.

But some of us on crystal days
know better than to stand in one spot,
once reflection coaxes us
to dare the one task
we were born to do;
to break through ice, plunge into water
and be.

And you can't be in one place.

I yielded native ground to discipline at 61,
having learned to think on purpose
takes more effort than I'd ever given,
and more courage than imagination.
Now, immune to fear, I peer
beneath this image of myself
to plumb blue depths,
having become
a happy hamster running
inside wheels of thought,
traveling to all the worlds
that thought has dared take me.

My journey is the gift
being in thought has given me,
and, along with my children,
all I have to give the world.

A Great Hat

Often I attend events indoors.
Upon arrival, I pilgrimage to the coat rack
and deposit this hat upon the shelf above.
Then, I step back and compare my hat
with others surrounding it.

Always, other hats are more presentable than mine.
Always, other hats look nicer than my hat.
But, they're not nicer.
This is a great hat!

It's a great hat partly because of the skill of the hatter,
but primarily because it has Character.

Three things infuse a hat with Character.
First, your hand, and the thumbprint
only you impress upon it.
Second, your head, and the signature manner
hat and crown impress each other.
Third, and most important of all, your feet.

Because it's your feet that sally your hat into the world,
where sun bakes its edges;
where rain baptizes it;
where sleet and snow flavor and sauté it;
where tree branches test it, scar it,
and rudely knock it to the ground;

and where sometimes the hat lifts from your head
as if with a will of its own
to tumble along, racing a wind
it can never hope to defeat,
all the while morphing into a shape
that elements and low-hanging obstacles can never defeat.

So, if you want to bless your hat with Character,

first embrace it with your hand,
then grace it upon your head,
and finally, go somewhere
and do something to earn the right
to walk humbly beneath it.

A Prominent Impediment

I've always tried to make peace with my impediments.

Even as children we seldom fought.
Of course, there were the teenage years, but even then
a brother's love would heal rifts among us,
despite our differences.

As you can guess,
some days I refuse to be held back
at the same time my impediments won't budge,
so a few of us get angry at each other
and revert to our teenage years.
But we're learning.

We were watching football the other day
when a prominent impediment brought it up.

"Toward certain ways I'm simply not going
to budge," he said.

"I know," I said.
"It's just that some days you're blocking the way I'm going,
and I'm too boxed in to see a better route."

To this he said, "I get that. I can only say
once you find your way out of your box
we can continue to travel together
and you'll have near-infinite ways to choose.
Meanwhile, it's your problem to solve, man;
I've given you all the clues."

Revenge

I sometimes feel a thought
like something crawling up my leg.

I know it's not vegetable or mineral,
but there's not much else I'm sure of,
except that my cat eyes me from a distance,
ears back, tail twitching.

Think before you laugh.
Foreign thoughts can blow themselves up
in crowded places,
martyrs for a sinister cause. How

will we react? What damage might we cause?
How quickly can we recover from wounds
inflicted by the martyred thought
not to mention the damage we cause?

And most important of all,
will I find the faith to face
this thought that's crawling up my leg?

AWARENESS

"The more clearly you understand yourself and your emotions, the more you become a lover of what is."

– Baruch Spinoza

Faces in the Lake

On New Year's Day, I made this pledge in Phoenix:
"I resolve to pay attention."

Too many things I've overlooked from year to year.
I've only this winter discovered how water ripples
in time with each season's own rhythms.

Even this morning, a gladiator sun skating
its flaming chariot across the frozen lake,
I stood in the clearing overlooking the dam
and spied teal water rippling near the arboretum.

A quarter mile from where I stood, below a shelter,
a score of geese still-lifed upon a patch of open water,
their morning shadows on the shallows
reminding me of school-day friends. Now
I'm on a promontory overlooking a silent swimming beach.

I like to stroll along this cove,
beneath a favored hat, my shelter,
visiting silhouettes along the shoreline,
humming past honeysuckle, communing with oak,

and scrunching leaves now brown and crumbling,
dedicating their humus to a soil
that flinches as I step. There's white oak and elm.
I'm sure I'd spot maple if I were more attentive.

On the leeward bank, four half-grown nut trees strut,
never noticing crusted profiles in the surface just
beyond them. They seem to still be learning subtle things.

Perhaps they feel in their limbs
how the sun haunts the horizon too long
during midwinter mornings and evenings.
Perhaps they sense the elm and maple are their kin.

Perhaps they, too, admire the patience of the heron.

But if they had rooted on the lake's west side
in the shade of these chinkapins, their limbs
would sway above a higher shoreline as they watch

the score of geese launch out from open water, chanting
to summon courage for the journey they're beginning,
pledging their intentions to their friends reflecting in the
     lake.

Once past their hickory heifer years
they could lean toward the shaded campground,
where trunks and branches of a seasoned generation
glow golden in the evening sun.

Against their thickening armor,
they could feel this frigid gust rush
faster than their friend, the fox, can run.

Then they'd feel the joy come rippling with discovering
     why
faces in the lake seem older when the wind blows.

An Emerald Gift

I remember the mid-summer morning a hummingbird flew
whirring past me,
as I stood half-asleep and shivering in crisp mountain air,
reel in hand and hook in stream,
gambling my bacon breakfast with trout.

Entranced by twilight's colored quiet
and honey-suckled fragrance,
I was following misty fingers drifting upward,
escaping current,
when suddenly, the hummingbird.

On singing wings, she emerged
from gray cliffs behind me,
and, spotting me watching her,
delayed her greater purposes to play for me,
performing her aerobatics
as if noting some musical backdrop
for her own ballet.

Like a jester prancing for a prince
she pantomimed an ode
in praise of woods and water,
dashing around my fishing line,
skimming silvery upstream rapids,
rising to visit orange honeysuckle,
then finishing her supernal climb above an owl's nest
and hovering
like an emerald hung around the rising sun.

And when she was gone, I found myself
transfixed by the mountain scene:
behind me, steep, bending cliffs that bent the crystal
    stream;
before me, a bleached sand beach, its mottled sycamores
and blue-green woods beyond;

below me, rainbow-gilded trout;
and, in reflection, captured between things high and low,
me.

So Lucky

I fried an egg, over medium,
buttered toast with a bit of jam,
then savored.

Simple though it was, it was
the best breakfast I'd had in years,
not because of the egg
or toast
or butter
or jam
or even their combination,
but because I paid attention.

It's as hard as chewing nails to be aware
of all that's on my plate.
I suffer many days distracted
by the battle for my tongue
self-love wages with the world;
meanwhile, my appetite betrays the rest of me.

Today, the battle's on again,
but at least I have my chance
to fry this egg
butter toast
spread jam
then relish each flavor.

The egg should be so lucky.

Compared With All There Is

Snowflakes make me sometimes think in terms of
    macrocosmic splendor
much like an atom
seems self-similar to All There Is.

I admit, the mind can over-think analogies;
there are limits to conclusions we can draw.
Even what I am
compared with All There Is
probably is impossible to know.

Still, as I sit in my favorite pub drinking my favorite beer
my half-blind mind imagines All There Is
as mindful of its own splendor.
If that's true, whatever unfathomable reality might be,
it knows it's here.

Familiar Fragrance

To say "God is one" is to say God is everywhere,
and for good measure, everywhere aware.

I said that to a solemn fellow beneath a belfry
when I was in my teens;
he scratched beneath his collar
then suggested I leave the church.

Soon after vespers, I did,
followed a star I prayed might guide me home
and wound up here.

I suspect it doesn't matter
that no matter where we are
some familiar scent inhabits wherever that is
as we cross the moment's threshold.

We can sometimes feel the omnipresent hug
enveloping us, warming us,
inviting us to pause, close our eyes
to better enjoy the fragrance

and while trying to remain alert
to what little we can sense
have another chat with God.

Birds Over Water

Something in the sight of birds over water
soars beyond our dwelling
on the thought of it.

Know what I mean?

Whether swallows casting freely
geese in noisy clusters
or a solitary heron coasting low
with solemn purpose

some shimmering in the sight
of birds over water
easily glides above
whatever feelings, good or evil,
that seeing it excites in us.

Am I making any sense?

This presence sensed,
though neither thought nor feeling,
imprints itself
with foggy nod and feathery stirring.

Or am I just insane?

Just as love and logic
spring from mind and not our brains,
something quite apart from mind
hops a ride with it to visit us
whenever we see wings with purpose
sailing over water.

I don't have words for it.
I can't apologize for missing metaphors
or lack of proper feet to carry them.

We've all sensed something over water
that defies poetic eloquence.

I'd simply like to challenge you
next time you gaze upon a lake
to put yourself inside that bird you see
like a camera in the cockpit of a HobbyZone glider
carries you through clouds.

Then you'll feel no further need to feel
or wonder
as you ride that kindred spirit over water.

COURAGE

"Can you imagine the hopelessness of trying to live a spiritual life when you're secretly looking up at the skies not for illumination or direction but to gauge, miserably, the odds of rain?"

— Anne Lamott, *Traveling Mercies*

View from Smoky Hill

The view from Smoky Hill stretches unobstructed
by hickory, oak and maple.
In most directions, no Quixotic structures
stitch the landscape.
Nor does smoke obscure this prairie partially checked by
    plows.

Well, perhaps on certain days,
as winged, serpentine mist ranges
low above the languid river;
on pungent mornings when red-orange burns
eastern horizons where they collide
with lesser hills.
Then, predawn, Sir Dragon rises,
like the Flint Hills' patron saint,
intent on quenching foreign fires
before they scorch the West.

I understand the river's fear of losing its possession.
Still, unhindered by current, I
can turn the other way and see as much, or more,
and stretching even farther West
past unseen nascent mountains I can sense
an unplowed universe unveiling.

Reaching

I saw a little man standing on his deck and looking up,
following something speeding east to west
across the southern sky. I sensed him reaching
for a falling star
and standing taller for the try.

Mountain Climber

He climbed too close to sacred peaks.

On Sundays we would shake our heads
and let him know how mad it was
to scale edges. Once we heard
him joke about a scarcity
of air at rarer altitudes.
And several times we watched him pray
while dangling from a precipice.

So, no one feigned surprise that day
Emanuel collapsed near one
such sacred peak. But dying slowly
gave him time to find his voice
and reminisce about grand vistas
none of us had ever seen
while trailing lower altitudes.

Brazilians With Their Big Black Cats!

The wild-eyed lady at Sunnybrook
warned me about them.
Her nurse worried I might write an exposé.

And for good reason;
because it's my duty to warn my readers about
Brazilians with their big black cats!

Certainly they're a danger, aren't they?
At any rate, they'll make great front-page copy,
especially if I emphasize the
BIGNESS and BLACKNESS
of both the Brazilians and their cats!

Of course, it won't be my fault
if readers over-react. But when they do,
I will be embedded,
helmet snug and camera snapping,
on the front lines of defense against
Brazilians with their big black cats!

A Bit of Hobbit

I suppose I knew before I ever read about Baggins
there's a bit of Hobbit in each of us
a bit not the least interested in adventure
but, when unable to escape it
resolves to enjoy it.

Does ever there come a moment
when you no longer yearn to return to the Shire?
When you make your home in adventure?
What if a series of adventures lead you homeward?
Would you expect to find the shire you left behind?

I'm Just Saying

Imagine an amoeba becoming
a living soul.

Imagine the chasm
that cell patiently, persistently,
spirited from to become a soul.
Is that the measure of the chasm
you and I are emerging
from toward our next haven?

Now imagine the universe as a nest
of nests, and this new-born soul
has just moved into ours.
You know the joy of expectation.

Next, imagine the strands of courage
patience weaves,
and think of the strength coalescing
inside persistence's shell.

Finally, imagine in this nest of nests
awareness of a self
greater than your soul
that *is* your soul
because you are part of it
and have always been.

You also know such a soul
would love enough to let
you keep your sense of self
to be and move and act at will
while still, at will,
realizing yourself as all there is.

That's why I'm mentioning
just moments ago I watched

a heron alight upon an abandoned dock
and she seems inclined to stay
searching the water
for as long as it takes.

So, I'm just saying....

TRUTH

"A foolish consistency is the hobgoblin of little minds, adored by little statesmen and philosophers and divines. With consistency a great soul has simply nothing to do. He may as well concern himself with his shadow on the wall. Speak what you think now in hard words, and tomorrow speak what tomorrow thinks in hard words again, though it contradict every thing you said today. — 'Ah, so you shall be sure to be misunderstood.' — Is it so bad, then, to be misunderstood? Pythagoras was misunderstood, and Socrates, and Jesus, and Luther, and Copernicus, and Galileo, and Newton, and every pure and wise spirit that ever took flesh. To be great is to be misunderstood."

– Ralph Waldo Emerson, "Self-Reliance"

The Historical Record

I distinctly remember the way
the boat, gliding left to right,
flickered red and white
through low-hanging hickories,
its motor barely humming.

She remembers my shifting
line of sight disrupting
her communion with boat, lake and hickories,
and doing so loudly.

We also have differing recollections
of what happened in Atlanta
when Led Zepplin came to town.

We continually amaze each other
over how differently the other records each day.
But after all these songs we've sung together
we're not easily fooled into fighting
over which of us is out of tune,

because we've learned
to not too closely listen for disharmonies
so as to rejoice in our duet.

Sometimes a Story

We needn't take that treacherous trek
through the tale of Abraham almost murdering his son
once we've freed ourselves from lesser gods.
So why is it still commonly done?

Freud is said to have said
a cigar sometimes is just a cigar.
A story of the depth of a son's faith
is nothing more – the rest, detail.

I'm not a patient man, I confess.
I know there's merit in searching
for layers of fabric in stories;
meanwhile, the simplest message
comes up gold, an unassuming crown unburdened
by ruby and diamond.

In the end, logic wins
and you can enjoy a character-revealing story
like little George W. confessing about cherry trees
or perhaps boasting of his skill with an axe.
Sometimes a story's just a story.

Dr. Frankenstein's Muse

It woke me at midnight and grasped my hand,
towering above my bed, a multi-metamorphous hulk,
commanding me to quench its thirst
with an oil spill of words.

Trembling, I obeyed, quickly gathered all my pens,
and scribbling without hesitation,
watched it quaff its black draft down,
unaware of sweet or sour, never caring.

I poured out nonsense – gulped down in a flash,
mixed in some humor – gone without a laugh.
I fed it my most sacred dreams,
it never slowed to savor them,
but bellowed "More!" obscenely belching,
verbolts of lightning arcing its electrodes,
and cross-wits trivia, like quicksilver, drooling down its
        chin.

I milked my pens until my fingers ached,
rambling disconnected thoughts to quell its appetite,
hoping my reflexive wit could parry its desire.

Gradually, as its hunger seemed to dwindle with the dark,
I noticed its demeanor change,
and finer rhythms framed his voice,
bubbling Alpha's word-made-flesh
from the pool of his tar pit mind.

"Love is never blind," he said,
"but sees beyond the eye's distorted images,
groping for simplest truths
stripped of fabrics words have woven,
to perceive and pursue that passion for perfection
every lover longs for."

Then, as he bowed and beckoned toward my window,
stitches stretching with his grin,
he whispered, "Always upward! – Going my way?"
and left me, my unconscious mind unbound, wondering
as I drifted back to sleep.

Ethical Quandary

Is it sinful
for a writer to
deliberately
withhold information
from his muse?

If It Were True

I heard an old story played fresh on flute
to a tune that might have been too hard to sing...
     if it were true.

Then again,
there's truth and there's fact, siblings perhaps...
     but not twins.

In any event, that story has been countless times retold
without the flute, and so, the singer claims...
     has suffered greatly.

True enough, the flute seemed not to fully recognize
its old friend, thanks to changes in the narrative time...
     had cultivated.

But the flute, having been there, knows the original
better than the singer, and so is in the best position to...
     choose between the two.

Authority

In late September, I was twilighting on a park bench
on the west side of Lake Shawnee
facing a moon that wasn't full
but was close.
One or two days, one way or the other.

In any event
it was a bright moon
on an almost dark evening in a mostly clear sky;
may have been a little fog.
The moon's reflection rippled silver in the water,
a precious thing to see;
probabilities suggest you've seen it, too.
I live 100 yards from the lake
so I've visited the moon's reflection often.

But I've never seen such moonshine
as when, on this late September evening
a boat split that ripple of silver
exciting it with its wake
in the same instant several geese skied through the shine
with similar effect.

This happy happenstance created
several quivering slivers of silver
and I quivered sympathetically to its three-fold beauty.
And it felt good.
And it felt true.
And the fog enhanced it.

Do you believe me?
Do you think this actually happened,
or am I just making this up?

I will tell you this happened —

although I may have enhanced it.
Or perhaps not.
Perhaps there was no fog,
I'm really not sure.
In any event, I'm telling you, this happened.

Do you believe me?
What authority do you give my words?
Whether you choose to believe me
or choose not to
or choose not to hold an opinion
you commit an act of faith.
Just bear in mind that if I hadn't posed the question
probabilities suggest that most of you would not have
        thought to doubt me.

What is the Word of God?
Is it a book?
What gives a book authority?

I read a book I put more stock in
than any established canon.
Never mind what it is;
doesn't matter.
What this book says about God
has a balanced beauty to it.
And it feels good.
And it feels true.
And there's no fog.

Largely because of this book I believe
a fragment of God lives in each of us.
A holistic fragment;
think fractals.

If I'm right,
then it's possible for me to hear God's voice

from inside me.
Along with a lot of other voices,
a complicating factor.

In any event, I search for goodness, truth and beauty
and whenever I look inside a book, or inside me
or glimpse a ray of greater light reflected in the night
and feel quivering slivers of silver ripple through me
I accept its authority.
Science notwithstanding,
probabilities suggest you're inclined to do the same.

Of course, there are disciples of books
who would limit our religious freedom by proclaiming:
"This is the Word of God.
This book.
This book is the Word of God,
and if you don't believe that,
and don't believe every word in this book,
you have no future."

I know people of great faith
who have left churches, temples, mosques
and institutions of higher learning
rather than endure this blasphemy.
I know people of great faith
who have confused themselves as well as others
while struggling to accept it.

You don't have to accept it.
I can tell you from experience
you can find your quivering slivers of silver
as much in lunar light reflecting
and Whitman's leaves of grass
and especially that piece of God inside you
as in any established canon.

Do you believe me?

LOVE

"Do you know what is better than charity and fasting and prayer? It is keeping peace and good relations between people, as quarrels and bad feelings destroy mankind."

– Muhammad

In the Garden

A young woman in a satin wedding gown
at first seemed lost among the mums
and roses
until I spied the young man trailing.

He caught up as she entered a gazebo, white cloud
held by four white pillars,
and focusing on a fountain in a shallow pool,
they stopped to chatter.

Soon they stood in silence and in stillness,
learning even more about each other
from their silence
and from the fountain,
until she'd learned enough.

Turning, she surveyed
the mum path ahead, gray ribbon
meandering out of view.
He hesitated, gazed around the garden,
then glanced downward.

Glancing back, she smiled at him,
but his camera at that moment held his fancy.

Perhaps that's why she slid
one hand around a pillar
and, using it as pivot point, swung half-circle,
then flung her free hand from her lips
toward his lowered forehead.

This happened while he fiddled
with his one-eyed toy,
so he missed the buss she blew.
Looking down herself, she slowly turned
and glided up the ribbon out of view.

He regained his focus as she disappeared.
Head erect and eyes alert,
he may have guessed he'd missed love's token,
and he quickly followed.

Confidante

He revealed his gravest fears
then fell in love
with one who was listening.
The steel she found in knowing
she used to forge his brace
and she pressed him firmly
and he held her dearly.

My Muse's Challenge

My muse claims divine love is self-love perfected.
I've no good reason to believe
otherwise. I only know my own love
is an artless brush with tainted palette.

To be honest, my muse's challenge attracts me to a truth
that loves me, and so, has given me you.

As often as I wonder if this truth is fair,
I ponder how I've treated you for forty years.
I've had good days and bad.

I'll not waste what brush strokes I have left on promises.
Now is the wrong season for snow-bound resolutions.
Now is when leaves show their true color
and fruit ripen.

My Daughter the English Teacher

My daughter the English teacher
(except she's not a teacher yet
but soon will be)
sat in the back of our car, her taxi
to the airport, travel bag beside her,
Leaves of Grass balanced in her hands
chanting "Song of the Open Road."
And as I listened,
I loved her even more.

I don't like terminals.
Each time I watch her wing away from me
the sky goes empty
and earth pulls heavier on my feet.
This time, the only difference was the echo of her voice,
"Afoot and light-hearted, I take to the open road,
healthy, free, the world before me,"
and I wished her God-speed;
the sooner she found Berlin, the sooner
I could read her letters home
and love her even more.

Her letters home: Valentines
expressing her affection for her newest fellowship of love,
young students from each compass end,
all strangers in the city with the broken wall,
their golden cord
a yearning to learn another tongue.

She bracketed each profile of her friends with
        commentaries,
reminders that each of them is kin to me:
the girl from Texas, so proud of her country;
the young man from Tibet, wishing he still had one;
the Norwegian, too strange to be bound
to one flag;

the Israeli, the Egyptian and their fragile friendship;
the Brazilian, who taught them to dance;
the German, who soberly watched the news report
on genocide in Darfur;
the Italian who embraced each one;
and, mixing bubbly with them all, my charmer,
dancing while she cooked, until the news came on.

And as I read her expanding prose,
I loved her even more.

The day anticipated four months came sunny,
and I arrowed to the airport
to retrieve my daughter the English teacher
(except she's not a teacher yet but will be in a month).
As I waited by the gate
I heard her signature, love-the-world laugh
rolling through the tunnel
and I loved her even more.

But when the tunnel once more birthed her back to me,
I barely recognized her.
Her clothes spoke German without accent,
her face, kissed by foreign suns,
reflected continents I'd never touched,
her eyes were globes more full than when she'd left.
I knew at once those globes had turned my girlish traveler
into the woman who will one day teach your children well.

And as she turned her globes toward me and smiled,
I loved the world I saw.

Divine Reconciliation

Mistakes were made at every point
by every dot devoted to the plane
but that did not deter the plane
which stretched toward infinity
to grant each dot its spot to be
then blessed each one for its impression.

Love Glides

Love glides too nobly to be disrespected
even when unreturned – or worse – unrecognized.
Only in moments of insanity
do we wish to cripple Grace

as we sense her mystic gown
sweep, unseen, behind a corner.
We would have kissed her outstretched hand
had we turned around in time.

Even now, if we have the sense to follow
when we turn that corner
we will find her waiting,
smiling,

and we'll know that once again
we've already been forgiven.

Weathered Together

My hat and I have grown together
weathered together long enough
we can find each other in a crowd.

We came upon each other
just this past spring
at a Brian Wilson concert.
That's a story you and I can learn from,
about Al and Brian, life-long partners in song
a friendship that outlasted blood,
still onstage, that night, fifty years after first performing.

For a while blown apart by a storm,
now weathered back together by their harmony
voices blending and rising above the applause
finding each other in the crowd.

But I was talking about my hat, I think,
and vibrations we feel when we caress
that redefine us both.
Is that the touch of friendship?
Are we remolded from what we were into who we are
shaped in part by who we press close
when in the crush of the crowd?

A week after "Pet Sounds," we embraced
two honeymooners at a truck stop
their New Orleans home stolen by a storm
then blown to Kansas
weathered together further by four younger, fellow exiles
friendships formed from blood.

To what extent can pilgrims grasp the path beneath their
        feet?
Or trees sense soil supporting their roots?
My hat has shared travails with me,

secrets you will never know,
and oh, the secrets you could share with us, but never will
for love of friends you have found in the crowd.

Falling Sideways

I once watched foxes dancing in rain.

They didn't seem so nimble, really,
falling sideways sometimes,
colliding once or twice.

Perhaps apparent inadvertent bumps
are foxes' way of flirting,
much like you and I might pop
each other with our towels
after dancing in rain.

More intriguing was the falling sideways
not something you'd expect
from creatures celebrated for their nimbleness.
It made me feel less guilty for mistakes
I make while straining, in my intentional,
though awkward manner, to have fun.

I'm not implying that the towel pop was accidental;
it just never did occur to me that you might take offense.

With You in Mind

I wrote these words with you in mind
because I mostly love you.

He's here, you know,
right here, right now
and more than mostly loves you.

When I leave, he'll come with me
but also stay with you
because he loves us both,
and loves us more than "mostly."

Good Enough for God

Gravity aside, if a universe-sized diamond
were set inches from my nose
its enormity and nearness would confound me.

From such a disadvantaged vantage point,
I'd scarcely know its value
nor appreciate its beauty
but I would spy the flawed reflection in that perfect gem
then pray my sense of awe is good enough for God.

ETERNITY

"Fear not."

– Jesus, *Matthew 10:28, Matthew 10:31, Matthew 17:7, Matthew 28:10, Mark 5:36, Mark 6:50, Luke 5:10, Luke 8:50, Luke 12:4, Luke 12:7, Luke 12:32, John 6:20....*

Wake and Swell

Along with our spot at the top of the food chain
comes the task of taking good care
of the place where we live and the places we go
regardless of the pain.

This occurred to me while I was stranded in the rain.
Today, between Eden's wake and swell, we dance for
Ever After, singing and laughing as we go
regardless of the pain.

Suppose the Milky Way

Suppose the Milky Way can self-correct its spin until its
    revolution is complete.

Moving through eternity like a clock, its arms embrace
a different segment of the universal curve,
and, as if in faith, the galaxy begins another pirouette.

Our second time around, think of changes
we'll see among the pilgrim stars,
some gone, some new, ensuring our perspective
will never be the same.

If Sunday is the mirror of the week
window follows clear glass window through Saturday.
Along the curved Way, each flawed day
in turn, is tracked by fleets of stellar mariners,
whose GPS and charts are not enough
to pinpoint where the windows lie. In the end,
faith will guide them as they self-correct their spin
through this galactic sea.

So does the universe evolve to justify
its own eternity -- by attenuating time
and circumstance to fine-tune every world.
When Sunday comes again,
I pray the day's reflection
will find an honest man.

Moss on Aspen

It happens as often as moss on aspen.

It begins with a presence he senses
before it impresses his senses. Next,

quivering aspen leaves
prompt him to listen,

so that he can't in good conscience
continue about his business. Then,

he spreads himself beneath these branches, contemplates
my single root beneath this stand of aspen, and

he's there! Soft, moist, much like space
inside caves, it curls around him

and he divines from carvings on the walls
his own meaning.

Finally, he comes to me for advice;
out of grace I pretend I don't know why,

and he tells me in ways that sanctify my listening.

Full Blossom at Damascus

What seeds are these, discharging from Virgo's quasar,
purling from its ever expanding vortex?
What pristine dewdrop primes their push
toward noon's intensity,
bursting forth to cupel light,
to mine rich ground around us?

Intuitive to me, this sense of buds unfolding.
The miracle of seeds is that their molds confirm
the future, myriad-mixed and unpredictable,
as osmotic spasms
tirelessly probing soil and space.

Blossom for me at Damascus,
star-bred lilac bush divine;
join me where this river's delta flips
broken, liquid images of twilight in reflection
to form an estuary for the morning after.

Let's whirl a vortex of our own,
and, weaving beard to whorling branch,
each path traverse entwined,
our blended spirit like a quasar glowing,
pioneering endlessness,
penetrating speed itself,
mocking space and time.

Setting Down My Kayak

I've been here before, many times,
carting my kayak up and down this beach
same as today. Moments from now
I will slide this simple vessel into shallow water
climb inside, push off and paddle away
leaving an impression in the sand.

So, never-mind the wolf's howling
over the supposed unreality of time.
The proof that something occurred before
whatever wake I'm about to make
is imprinted on this beach,

a beach a certain sequence helped me reach
just as another sequence will paddle me away
whatever the truth about time.

Always the Rhythm

Always the rhythm came first
laying the base for ears to hear
while serving as the poet's loom
to interlace melodies
onto the musical scale of the spoken word.

The word emerged from midnight
with its natural tones and harmony
as bride. Both were unaware of rhythm
until the morning's pink was passing,
then barely grunted their indifference.

Never was it clear precisely when
intention wrapped itself around them
to guide, then ride their liquid momentum.
But once they'd made arrangements
for a passage, listeners could hear
where they were going.

In time, they learned to work and play
together fairly, music fine-tuned
by enduring conversation,
while its melodies lent substance to the word.
They even learned to dance together
taking turns leading, seldom breaking cadence.

And so, the spoken word and music,
help-mates to each other
unconsciously devoted to the beat
composed their magnum opus.

They waved and bowed at their finale
graciously acknowledging applause
and in the silence where the spotlight greets the dust,
once again became aware of rhythm
gave thanksgiving to the rhythm

humbly accepted judgment from the rhythm
and rejoiced at the revelation
there would always be
the rhythm.

The Forgotten Fragment

No one would have suffered if I'd thrown it away,
but I kept it
lining a bottom drawer for twenty years
before computers. For twenty years more
it's flickered in and out of memory
yet never found its way into a Word file.

Well, here it is now.
What should we do with it?

About the Author

Duane Johnson is a retired journalist who treats his poetry as an oral art form. Lives in Kansas. Married to a social worker. Two grown children. Modest house with gray siding on a dead-end street. Chain saw, fishing gear and kayak in the garage. And the nearby 400-acre lake and surrounding woods is his laboratory. More meditations to come.

Connect with Duane R Johnson:

Facebook:
https://www.facebook.com/evolutionspromise/
Website:
http://www.viewfromsmokyhill.com/evolutionspromise